ARIES HOROSCOPE 2023

Alina A. Rubi

Alina Rubi

ISBN: 9798839356160

Independently Published

Edition: Alina A. Rubi and Angeline A. Rubi

rubiediciones29@gmail.com

Who is Aries?

Dates: *March 21 – April 19*

Day: *Tuesday*

Color: *Red*

Element: *Fire*

Compatibility: *Leo, Libra, Sagittarius, and Aquarius*

Symbol:

Modality: *Cardinal*

Polarity: *Male*

Ruling planet: *Mars*

House: *1*

Metal: *Iron, steel*

Quartz: *Red jasper, Rubi*

Constellation: *Aries*

Personality of Aries

The sign of Aries is the first of the zodiac, these are the people who always project themselves into the future but considering the experiences of the past.

People with high concentration of Arian energy in their natal charts are active and energetic. They are always on the move; they are very independent, and they are leaders par excellence.

They like to take initiative and compete with others to assess their skills. They often state how competent they are in emergency situations, as that is where they can evaluate their energies.

Aries do speak plainly, they go straight to the point and have a steely will to take risks with a lot of courage, since they have a lot of confidence in themselves. The difficulties for them do not exist, and they are always full of optimism in the face of any challenge that life throws at them; They are motivated to explore unknown territories and start projects from scratch, although they usually lose motivation once the first phase passes.

They need goals to pursue in which to invest their energies, although they are not persistent. Their aggressiveness is one of the characteristics that helps them in some situations, but in others it annihilates them because it blinds them. They share the optimism and enthusiasm characteristic of the other fire signs: Leo and Sagittarius.

It is considered the most energetic sign of the zodiac, always ready to fight against any obstacle that stands in their way, they do not cling to the past, nor do they warm their heads thinking about things that have no solution.

Its most outstanding positive characteristics are joy, optimism, autonomy, strength, initiative, and selflessness.

Being stubborn is one of their weaknesses, they are not easy to convince, even if you show it, they are very persistent. When they put themselves in this state, they are inflexible and self-centered. If something or someone crosses their path and arouses suspicion or annoys them, they will quickly change their mood and will not give in easily.

Aries General Horoscope

General

Aries begin a new chapter in your life in 2023. With your enthusiasm, and with Jupiter, the lucky planet in your sign until May 2023, all the projects you start will bring you success and prosperity. At the beginning of this new cycle there is a probability that you will change professions, or jobs.

You must enjoy your luck and show that you are up to all the opportunities that come into your life. It is wise to be ready to act when opportunities come.

If you need help, ask your colleagues or family members. This year you have a mission to fulfill, and you will gain many experiences, do not let them judge you, try to do everything right so that you do not give rise to this. Try to give structure to your life, so you will motivate others. Plan and use new strategies. Do not get lost in trivial things, try to be assertive and do not procrastinate.

As the year begins, there is an extraordinarily strong cosmic activity at important points in your natal chart. Jupiter transits through your sign, this is the perfect time for new beginnings, projects, opportunities, and trips. You can take the opportunity to do anything new and take the initiative for whatever you want. You can be more optimistic about life and feel good about your possibilities. Pluto is undermining your area of the profession by freeing you from projects that have no purpose.

The first eclipse of the year happens in your sign on April 20, this is the first solar eclipse in your sign since March 2006, you will have to set more solid goals. This eclipse happens in a sensitive place, for that reason it has a higher energy than usual.

There is a chance that you will feel motivated or anticipate future events and then not worry. Do not let follies be your ruin. A similar solar eclipse happened in the same position in your sign in April 2004, look at what events happened in your life at that time to get an idea of what could happen now.

Love

Adventure is synonymous with your name this year if you are looking for the ideal partner. Jupiter in Aries this year is activating the search for your twin flame. Your mood will be great if you are single, and you will create exclusive moments.

Your affable nature will put you in the environment of potential partners from all levels of society. One of those people will captivate your heart, and you will put it on a pedestal when you feel that the level of certainty and tolerance is mutual.

Notably, you will be on an exploration to discover the habits and attributes that this potential partner possesses, and as you get to know them, you will absorb with fascination all the fidelity and romance that this person offers you.

Your fiery spirit aspires to share love with someone compatible, who of course must be tolerant and accommodating to you. Anyway, although you are super quick to get irritated, this person will teach you to calm down, and you can reconcile and enjoy many moments of love.

The asteroid Ceres transits your area of relationships, in early 2023. This transit will help you to be more affectionate and responsible with the people who are part of your life, you can nurture your relationships if you are in a couple. You will be overly concerned about the people closest to you, both personal and professional, and you will try to feel that you are getting something important out of them.

Ceres will make its retrograde move from February to the end of March in this area, and this can be a period that gives you the opportunity to reflect on what you need to improve, or what you need to let go.

Venus also assesses your relationships in 2023 when it transits retrograde through your area of love, this happens after the first half of May until July. This transit will cause ruptures or conflicts that you will have to resolve. You can also develop a tendency to secret relationships. Enjoy, but do not neglect other areas of your life that will demand a lot of attention from you. Examine deeply whether it is in your interest to indulge in unbridled passion or whether it needs to be moderated.

Focus on communicating correctly and having healthy relationships. This way everything will flow, and you will not create karma. Retrograde movements are great for reconnecting with relationships that have been neglected recently.

Ceres returns to your relationship sector from the end of June to the middle of September, to make the corrections that were left pending. Mars, take a walk from late August to mid-October, through your area of love, and you will feel motivated to commit.

On October 14, a solar eclipse comes to your engagement area, giving you opportunities for new relationships, renewing existing ones, or meeting new people. With this Eclipse there is the possibility of being offered a second job. You may be presented with opportunities that involve working for or with others.

Another Eclipse, but this one is Moon, happens in your love section on May 5th. If you have problems buried in your subconscious this is the perfect time to face them, specifically those related to intimacy. You will feel the need to get away from a person with whom you no longer have connection, and you must do so if you want to move forward on your path.

You will have the opportunity to strengthen your emotional bonds from September to November when Mars your ruling planet and Ceres re-transit your relational area.

Aries, although you have not had the best moments in love recently, since you had to put aside relationships to take care of work and other important matters, this year 2023 is going to make you feel the real dimension of your isolation.

It is imperative that you reconnect with your friends, your partner, and the people you need by your side. Try to reconstruct what you left aside.

Economy

Being the center of attention is not your strongest part, however, you will be phenomenally successful in your professional area when you present your creative ideas. Your plans will be so solid that everyone around you will risk investing with you.

You will discover strategies to solidify your projects and have skills that no one else has in business. Just remember that being impulsive is your weak point, for that reason keep going, but do not act rashly. If you fall into the trap of your impulses, you will have to start from nothing each project and you will fall behind.

Here the key is to finish what you start, one day at a time, one thing at a time. Do not feed a lot of new ideas that make you lose sight of your goals. If this happens you will become aggressive with your co-workers and your family.

It will be a very prosperous year for you. You have already experienced a bit of lack the previous two years, and now you know how you should behave and save.

Pluto will be transiting through your professional area, it feels hard because it has been there for almost ten years, it leaves at the end of March for a while, it re-enters in mid-June, and it stays for the rest of 2023. You should already know that Pluto wants you to define yourself, that's why life turns your upside down, because it wants you to change direction and clarify your goals. If you have not done it in the last decade, important transformations await you at a professional level.

Mercury is retrograde in early 2023, until mid-January in your section of the profession, and will be retrograde briefly in mid-December. This can generate energy for you to do anything you have not yet achieved.

The three retrograde periods of Mercury this year affect your professional area, and therefore your finances. Pluto wants you to take more control, and Mercury will help you take the reins or destroy yourself. Traditionally, this is a good opportunity to make a career change, look for ways to earn more money, or change work schedules.

Beware of fraud and conflicts with the authorities in your workplace. Permanence is not typical of retrogrades, even if you feel happy in the way your life is in that area, try to focus on making small adjustments. If you hate what you do, you will hate it even more. Be smart about it.

The asteroid Ceres in retrograde motion also influences your economic area from the end of March to the beginning of May, it joins with Mercury in this task and all these energies will make you not feel focused on what you do.

You will also feel like you are not getting paid enough or what you deserve for your work, or that you are being given too much responsibility. Anything you are doing with disgust will be affected.

Mars comes to help you in the economy from mid-July to the end of August and will give you the energy you need to look for a job that you like or excite. This vibration is perfect for new projects and job opportunities.

Anyway, financially you will get a lot of financial help with Jupiter moving through your area of finance in mid-May. Jupiter joins Uranus in Taurus, which has been at that point for some years now.

Uranus has pushed you to make big changes, and Jupiter now comes to reward you for your efforts. You will see a lot of pleasant financial surprises for the work you have done correctly, and projects that have been paralyzed will move. You should be smart and cautious when Mercury retrograde transits your finance area in late April through mid-May.

A Lunar Eclipse on October 28 shakes your economy. If you acted thoughtlessly, this may be a time of adversity, however, with the favor of Jupiter, it is nothing serious.

People who are unemployed should not lose hope if they do not find work, because things are quite weak at a general level. They will have more opportunities after July so they should have their eyes open to the offers that are published.

What they should do is take advantage of that time to take classes that open more doors in the labor market. Its economy in general will strengthen during this year, and they will be able to give themselves small tastes and pay the monthly payments without stressing.

Family

Family relationships will be compromised, if you want to avoid difficulties it is important to have a sincere dialogue, making others understand that you are not able to fulfill all the claims. Friends will help you understand this moment you are living and will propose you to share your experiences with them. Despite needing moments of solitude to meditate, she finds time to accept her company. You will not regret it.

Mars in the family area from mid-March to mid-May, will make you feel motivated to focus on family. You may want to spend more time at home, move, redecorate, or renovate.

If you have children, Venus retrogrades from mid-May to mid-July in the sector that governs your children, you will make it more rebellious, and you will need a lot of patience. They may need your support for a challenging problem, and you can help them feel more protected.

Health

You will be prone to fights that will create stress, and a lot of frustration, especially at the beginning of the year when Mars retrograde plays with your mind.

You may face mental problems, or past traumas. Mars will be doing its thing in this area until the end of March. Then you will have time to replenish your mind and restore your positive focus.

In mid-November, Mars, and Mercury partially retrograde in your area of mind, give you energy for great ideas, projects, and optimism. With Mercury retrograde, you will need mental distance from others. Neptune has been in this area for a while and will continue to help you connect with your subconscious mind and let go of the past. Your intuition will be strong. Saturn transits this sphere in the first days of March and will stay the rest of the year. Think seriously about how to deal with your shadows and let go of some baggage. Saturn in this area is a stage for a deep cleansing of your mind and soul. Focus on understanding your past.

Overall physical health is good, but you can strengthen it by giving more attention to your bones. You may want to visit a chiropractor. It is paramount that your spine and overall posture are well aligned.

Advise

You must divest yourself of things or conceptions that no longer work. Discard your family or cultural conventions that, at one stage, were given to you but no longer work.

Do not be afraid to question. It is valid to be inexperienced in life, but if you do not ask people will accept that you know something that is not real, and then you will fail because you are incompetent. When you do not know the answer to something, always ask. As simple as the question is, do not be afraid to ever want to learn more.

You must watch your back because hidden enemies may be undermining your plans and trying to damage your image. If you have problems or any other issue that slows down your professional advancement, it is time to face it.

Get enough rest, a tired mind is a useless mind. Personal economy is important so you must instruct yourself how to plan, and of course comply with it fully. Beware of stock market speculation during this year, protect yourself.

It is important that you think seriously about how to take care of your health and eating habits, leave a little alcohol, and tobacco. If you do not do it in the time that Saturn transits through your house of health, the planet of karma will pass you the bill. Do not tie yourself to your archaic ways, incorporate the necessary reforms and assume them with confidence.

Aries Monthly Horoscopes 2023

January 2023

You start the month, and the year, regular because your ruling planet Mars, is retrograde. There will be many conflicts in your home that will hinder family ties. After the 18th everything starts to fix, and you will feel more relieved. Try not to argue with your partner because otherwise things will get worse. In the end, we all have different opinions and just because they share life does not mean they do not have a life of their own.

You will live nights of sex and passion if you are single, after the 11th, and you will feel in the clouds with so much love and eroticism.

You have a particularly good chance of getting a new job if you start looking after the 18th. Also, any business or project that was paralyzed will be completed and you will feel incredibly happy, plus you will earn a lot of money.

Anyway, you should be with your eyes open because there are other business opportunities in your way, you will receive the signals, but if you are entertained you will not notice.

At the end of the month things get complicated for those who are in a couple for a professional matter, they may have to separate for a while, and this will create a bit of chaos since love at a distance will make them meditate on the relationship and the problems they have and have ignored. Try to be patient because all couples have problems, take advantage of the distance to improve yourself physically, so your partner will find you more attractive when he returns.

You must watch what you eat because you are at risk of your blood pressure being decompensated. You do not want to bring your body to the same rhythm as your mind that is impossible.

You must be patient because there are many challenges in the coming months, so get used to being tolerant.

Lucky numbers
12, 23, 35, 39, 42

February 2023

Couple love should be a shared burden. You must not be thinking that the things that happened to you in the past are going to repeat themselves now. If you feel that you have traumas that come from the past it is time to go to therapy, or practice meditation to cleanse your subconscious of all that has your mind clouded with so much jealousy. After February 5, your partner may want to separate because you have her overwhelmed with so much control.

Trust is the first rule to be committed, otherwise you must be alone. What you are doing is selfishness you must remove all those ghosts from your mind so that you are happy.

Many problems between your partner's relatives and yours because they do not agree on something that has to do with the two families after the 14th, something related to where to spend the day of love and friendship.

Finally, they will agree and have a great time.

If you are single and dating more than one person, be careful because a difficult situation is in your way. The two people could meet because of some mistake of yours when reconciling the dates. They show up at your house and you have a big scare.

You must remember that you are not right in everything when a problem happens with a work colleague at the end of the month Learn to listen to advice and control that tendency of always wanting to win.

It is particularly good for you to treat yourself to a massage or go to the beach so that you can have a little energy. Breathing the sea air will be a perfect medicine for your stress.

You must be noticeably clear in your mind of what you want for your life because if you do not set goals, you will never get anywhere.

You will get money from speculation, a salary increases, or from some game of chance. Do not spend because a bit of tense times is coming in finance.

Lucky numbers
3, 14, 19, 22, 37

March 2023

You need to be calm, this month you are beginning to present patterns of anxiety, for issues that you have not been able to solve. If you get decompensated you will end up affecting the relationship with your *partner, and with your work colleagues.*

Spend a little energy cleaning your home, an energy cleaning is recommended. Also light a white candle on your doorstep and see how you start to feel better.

Already this month is less restrictive and controlling in love, and more considerate. You already have more desire to share, take advantage and go out to dinner with your partner, spend romantic nights after the 15th that the planets are blessing you.

If you are planning to have children this month is ideal, so plan nights of eroticism and passion so that you can conceive a child with a lot of love.

Remember that it is always healthy to admire the landscape around you, you can always find beauty, even looking at the stars at night.

There are changes and disorders, in your life at the end of the month, you must take care of accidents. If this happens, stay calm because it will not be anything serious.

In your workplace there are some changes that can affect you because the people in authority are going to change. You shut your mouth and do not make any comments because you are in danger of being involved in a comment that in the future may affect you.

Health must be taken care of, avoid drastic changes in temperature because your lungs can get sick. You need to analyze what you eat. A balanced diet is imposed so that you control cholesterol.

Try to have fun with your friends, plan meetings at home.

If you are single, you have opportunities for love at work, the traditional office romance.

In the area of business, your patience will be evaluated at the end of the month since a project does not advance as quickly as you would like. There is not much you can do about it, continuing to work is the solution.

Lucky numbers
15, 21, 32, 36, 41

April 2023

You prioritize your partner this month. You will put her on a pedestal with so many attentions, and she will be very flattered.

If you are single, you have opportunities to meet someone who may be your soul mate. It is someone related to your profession, or you know it on social networks.

If you have been thinking about taking out loan or credit, you are likely to get a negative response.

You should not start any new business until next month, nor invest large amounts of money. You will be tempted to make extra expenses that are not within your budget, always think: I like it, I want it, but I do not need it.

Remember that to succeed you must stay focused.

Lucky numbers
9, 14, 19, 23, 65

May 2023

You start the month quickly and with the energy of a superhero. You must follow your hunches, combine them with this energy and you will be extraordinarily successful in a project that has been delayed.

You can control your fate, create the conditions you need, the results will be positive after the second half of the month. Do not overdo it in wanting to control everything, because this can bring domestic problems.

If you are single, love tracks you ardently and at the end of this month, it will find you. You are likely to find love in charitable or religious groups, or as a volunteer in a just because you believe.

The financial aspect is excellent at the end of the month and your intuition remains strong. Moments of important changes, you not only have the possibility of improving your economic situation, but of gaining in personal security.

Bet on your creativity, everything is in your favor, but do not take unnecessary risks, since your character is prone to that.

Channel your energy by exercising but take care of your bones. If you get headaches, you may be developing migraines.

The shadow of infidelity appears again in your head. However, your partner has a lot of patience and will be tolerant of you.

If you planned a trip there may be delays or cancellations. You do not have to be alarmed, this change will not affect you, on the contrary, it is positive that it has happened.

Lucky numbers

7, 11, 13,26,40

June 2023

They will give you a lot of desire *to go out and visit new places, make new friends, and have fun. It is a stimulating month, full of dedication to the things you love.*

It will free you *from pressures, and it will also increase your interest in your inner development. Your creativity will be at the top and you will have many ideas of how to do business that can bring you a lot of profits in the future. Enthusiasm will escort you in everything you execute, and this will help you overcome any challenge.*

If you need help at work, you can ask your colleagues for it, and if others ask you, help them. Do not get involved in power struggles as you will end up in a powerful conflict with a fierce enemy that can make your life very bitter.

Plan a break to think about what you want to do, after the 22nd and include in your plans rigorous measures in the management of your expenses.

It is essential that you do not mix personal matters with work. Do not let your emotions cloud your reason, if it happens, you will lose a lot of money.

If you assimilate this the horizon will be clearer for you and you will know exactly what to do.

Lucky numbers
6 - 22 - 30 - 33 - 35

July 2023

Love and money haunt you this month, and after the 3rd you will be blessed by the planets. Your partner will be a bit complicated at work and this can create conflicts at home because you will have to take care of household chores.

This month you must be careful with all the documents you sign. There are people in your workplace who will try to trap you to harm you because they are envious of your active personality. Your best defense is to be tolerant, but still watch what you sign.

After the 19th you will want to improve your physical appearance, you may want to plan cosmetic surgery, or change your clothes closet. Any purchase you make in this period will be excellent.

You must learn to listen more to the people around you, they are more experienced people who want to help you not make the mistakes they already made.

If you are single, this month is the perfect opportunity to ask the right questions of the person you are meeting. You will realize that they do not have that much in common, and this will disappoint you, but do not worry that your soulmate is on its way.

Start making plans to take a vacation next month, if you do not have a partner you can go with your friends.

Remember not to stop doing the things you like just because your partner or family member has asked you to. Love is not about forbidding the other to enjoy the things he loves, but about strengthening talents.

Lucky numbers
10 - 13 - 26 - 28 - 30

August 2023

The first fifteen days of the month you will be extremely nervous because you have a lot of work, and you want to go on vacations at the end of the month.

Think and correctly evaluate each step you take, when you cannot do things alone, seek the advice of your friends, who will be by your side throughout this month.

It is not a month of much to compression between established couples since they are exposed to live secret adventures.

It is important, for those who already have established a relationship of time that they think twice before making a false step.

Singles will enjoy adventures and transient romances, do not forget about sexual protection measures because they can be contaminated with a venereal disease.

As for finances, do not be discouraged, nor do you lose patience. Try to be cautious and do not risk it, so you will not suffer disappointments.

Some friendships that no longer suit you leave your life.

It is important that you learn to know people well before receiving them with such joy.

Someone you love very much is thinking about physically hurting yourself, you may want to attract attention, but do not stop giving it importance, you should always worry about the *safety of the person you love.*

.

Lucky numbers
1 - 4 - 12 - 19 - 20

September 2023

This month you should stay calm. It is possible that you get entangled in an overly complicated situation, it does not mean that you will have serious problems, in fact, it is something that you can solve because you have nothing to do with the matter.

It is not a good mis to confess love to that person you like. That person does not feel the same as you and you will feel incredibly sad if you do. You must not dare to say what you feel, at least this month.

A change on a subconscious level will happen in you, due to emotional and family issues.

The planetary aspects are spectacular for buying or selling a home.

Forget that project that did not work, it is better that you see the page and throw the book, you should rest for a while and leave business or concentrate on another type of work.

You are waiting for a response from something you were promised and that makes you anxious. However, that news that you are looking forward to so much will not arrive until next month. You must be very calm because you have done everything in your power to get what you want, now is the time to leave things in the hands of destiny and focus on other goals. What you want will come now.

Lucky numbers
15 - 22 - 24 - 29 - 31

October 2023

Speculation is very favorable this month, but never act blindly.

You will be able to increase your self-esteem and gain experiences.

In love, your partner will ask you for definitions. Your partner has long said his desire to have children and consolidate the relationship. You have responded with evasiveness; however, this month will demand an answer.

You are likely to be attracted to spirituality.

You will also have to face issues in your life that you may have tried to hide and that are controlling you. Everything is resolved the moment you manage to identify what and assume that you are not guilty of any kind.

At the end of the month, you will receive a formal invitation to go out with friends that will be beneficial to generate new contacts.

If you think you have a rough patch or luck, do activities that tell you otherwise.

You get the news that they are going to return money they owe you.

Lucky numbers
11 - 12 - 14 - 20 - 31

November 2023

This month you must be strong because you were the one emotionally manipulated by your family. Try to be calm and listen to them patiently without being manipulated.

Do not be so demanding of yourself because this can cause you a lot of stress. You should also take care of joint pain, and this happens because the body asks you to rest.

There are several ways to relax, exercising is the main one, but meditating is important.

The intuition you have will help you generate money, if you continue to be guided by it you will be quite successful.

At the end of the month a person who has a lot of prestige wants to share his successes with you. Inviting you out, it is not a romantic outing, but a time to talk about business. You must catch up with technology so that your business continues to grow, try to pass suitable courses or that can contribute you with new ideas.

Some who have been with their partners for a long time will feel bored and although the relationship is stable, you miss the passion of the beginning. Relationships are based on stages, and all have their good things, enjoy everything that life gives you to share with this person.

Lucky numbers
7 - 9 - 10 - 29 - 32

December 2023

The love between your parents and siblings will be overly complicated by financial matters. Dislikes, especially after the 5th, will be the highlight of your life.

You are in a stable economic moment, but soon some typical year-end debts will arrive. Organize your economy and you will be able to face any scenario that arises.

If you are getting to know someone, do not be afraid to tell the truth to the person you are dealing with, take off your masks, and if by chance you have hidden something from him, it is time to be sincere and leave in his hands the decision to continue.

The fruits of your labor begin to progress and expand, you may see that life has many more good things on the way for you.

An old love from the past could cause you a problem when she unexpectedly shows up at a party where you will be with your partner.

If you want to maintain good health, you should drink more water to clean your system. You must keep your emotions controlled so that your sleep patterns do not lose their rhythm. Breathe fresh air.

At the end of the month and the year you will not pay attention to some important things because you will let yourself be carried away by the spirit of the holidays.

Get away from everything that distracts you, from social fantasies, use your mental power to grow your way. Focus your strength and energy on getting the abundance you deserve.

Lucky numbers

1 - 12 - 19 - 20 - 21

The Tarot Cards, an Enigmatic and Psychological World.

The word Tarot means "royal road", it is an ancient practice, it is not known exactly who invented card games in general, nor the Tarot in particular; There are the most dissimilar hypotheses in this regard.

Some say that it arose in Atlantis or Egypt, but others believe that tarots came from China or India, from the ancient land of the Romani people, or that they came to Europe through the Cathars. The fact is that tarot cards exude astrological, alchemical, esoteric, and religious symbolisms, both Christian and pagan.

Until recently some people if you mentioned the word 'tarot' it was common to imagine a gypsy sitting in front of a crystal ball in a room surrounded by mysticism, or to think of black magic or witchcraft, today this has changed.

This ancient technique has been adapting to the new times, has joined technology and many young people feel a deep interest in it.

The youth have isolated themselves from religion because they consider that there, they will not find the solution to what they need, they realized the duality of this, something that does not happen with spirituality. Throughout social networks you find accounts dedicated to the study and readings of the tarot, since everything related to esotericism is fashionable, in fact, some hierarchical decisions are made considering the tarot or astrology.

The remarkable thing is that the predictions that are usually related to the tarot are not the most sought-after, what is related to self-knowledge and spiritual advice is the most requested.

The tarot is an oracle, through its drawings and colors, we stimulate our psychic sphere, the most recondite part that goes beyond the natural. Several people turn to the tarot as a spiritual or psychological guide since we live in times of uncertainty, and this pushes us to look for answers in spirituality.

It is such a powerful tool that it tells you concretely what is going on in your subconscious so that you can perceive it through the lens of a new wisdom.

Carl Gustav Jung, the famous psychologist, used the symbols of tarot cards in his psychological studies. He created the theory of archetypes, where he discovered an extensive sum of images that help in analytical psychology.

The use of drawings and symbols to appeal to a deeper understanding is frequently used in psychoanalysis. These allegories are part of us, corresponding to symbols of our subconscious and our mind.

Our unconscious has dark areas, and when we use visual techniques, we can reach different parts of it and reveal elements of our personality that we do not know. When you manage to decode these messages through the pictorial language of the tarot you can choose what decisions to make in life to create the destiny you really want.

The tarot with its symbols teaches us that there is a different universe, especially today where everything is so chaotic, and a logical explanation is sought for all things.

Four of Pentacles, Tarot Card for Aries 2023

Tranquility will come to your life. You will be able to have peace and an organized life. You will know how to take care of yourself and that will help you stay healthy. It predicts a good balance of money, in fact, if you have an organized budget, it will help you maintain a great economic stability, achieving as results many profits. It is the perfect period for a business as luck is on your side.

Runes of the Year 2023

Runes are a set of symbols that form an alphabet. "Rune" means secret and symbolizes the noise of one stone colliding with another. Runes are a legendary visionary and magical method.

The runes do not serve for exact predictions, but they do serve to guide you on a future event, a topic, or a decision. The runes have a specific meaning for the person who wants it, but also some message related to the adversities that arise in life.

Fehu, Rune of Aries 2023

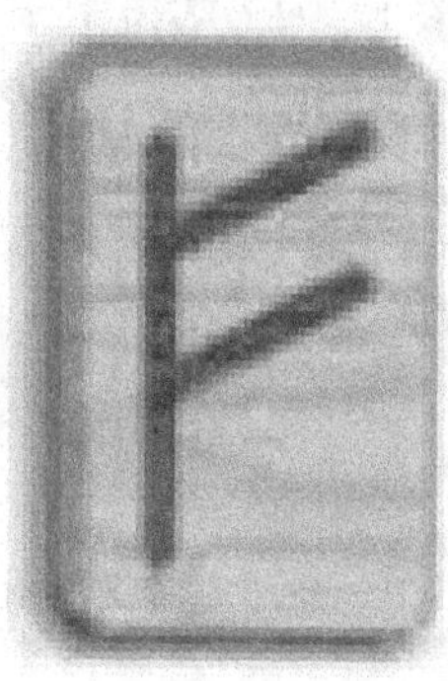

This rune will bring prosperity to your life, indicates material fertility, you can get everything you propose, and you will have a lot of peace in the sense of economy. You will get many rewards because you will try.

If you have been looking to have children, you will get it. If you want to start new projects you will do it, and you will be phenomenally successful because you will receive unexpected help.

It represents a love reciprocated, where the couple's relationship is solid and harmonious. As her deity Freyja, the Viking goddess of love, she prophesies a prosperous future in matters of the heart.

You can trace the rune Fehu, use its symbol as an ornament, place it as wallpaper on your phone, or computer, because it is the rune of prosperity, therefore, having it present will attract its energies.

It symbolizes economic benefits, and wealth. You will have to share with others. It indicates the beginning of a good period, where you will have short-term financial benefits.

At work comes a pleasant stage, with achievements of your goals. If you do not currently work, predict job interviews.

Lucky Colors

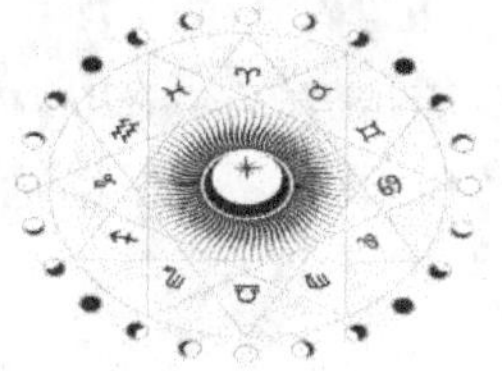

Colors affect us psychologically; They influence our appreciation of things, opinion about something or someone, and can be used to influence our decisions.

The traditions to receive the new year vary from country to country, and on the night of December 31 we balance everything positive and negative that we live in the year that leaves. We begin to think about what to do to transform our luck in the new year that is approaching.

There are several ways to attract positive energies to us when we receive the new year, and one of them is to wear or wear accessories of a specific color that attracts what we want for the year that is going to begin.

Colors have energy charges that influence our lives, so it is always advisable to receive the year dressed in a color that attracts the energies of what we want to achieve.

For that there are colors that vibrate positively with each zodiac sign, so the recommendation is that you wear clothes with the tonality that will make you attract prosperity, health, and love in 2023. (You can also wear these colors throughout the rest of the year for important occasions, or to enhance your days.)

Remember that, although the most common is to wear red underwear for passion, pink for love and yellow or gold for abundance, it is never too much to attach in our outfit the color that most benefits our zodiac sign.

Lucky Color for Aries

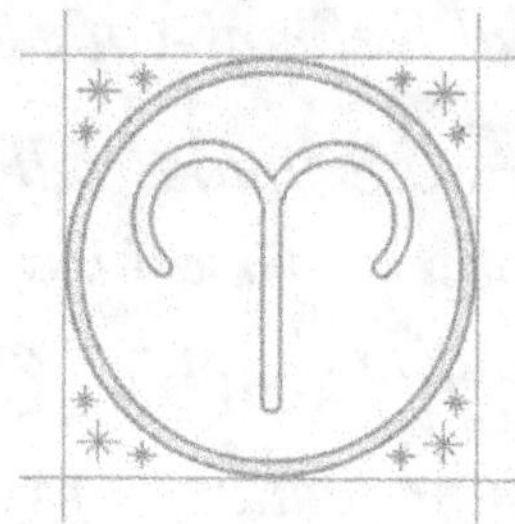

Yellow.

It is hard to ignore yellow, and if the hue is like gold, it projects prosperity. It is the color of intelligence, and it can help you think clearly.

The yellow is bright and clear, lightening everything it touches. It is the color of the Sun, so it symbolizes satisfaction, will, creativity and a sum of new feelings and joy.

It is an effective color on a psychological level, and could regulate blood pressure, blood sugar levels, cleanse your intestines, relieve arthritis, and heal your skin. It serves to balance emotional problems, specifically when we have negative obsessive thoughts.

It is the best color to use when we want to change negative parts of our personality, since yellow is cheerful, transferring more objective nuances to our mental attitude.

Your digestive system can be purified with yellow rays. You should pause from your daily routine and go out to spend a few minutes each day in a place where you can feel the sun's rays. You will feel how your body becomes more energetic.

Pour water into a yellow glass and place it in sunlight for half an hour. Drink this water while you focus on cleansing your body, mind, and heart.

The main features of yellow are its radiance, and luminous particularity. Yellow is expansive and uninhibited, so it helps in relaxation. Offering a yellow rose is synonymous with friendship, and the offering of a new beginning.

The hue of the air element is yellow. It intensifies mental talents and thought processes, therefore, any idea that is illogical or unreasonable, is eliminated when you use this color.

To manifest in the material world, this is the best color as it illuminates the mysteries of the conscious and subconscious mind. It stimulates the faculties of the mind, allowing it to work like a sponge.

People who have yellow color in the aura are full of joy and inner peace. These people are not tied to anything, or anyone, and they are always kind. A halo around the yellow head symbolizes a spiritual master. For holistic therapists, yellow is the color of peace, and it is the color of the Solar Plexus chakra.

The quartz that represents yellow are citrine, amber, and topaz.

*Within the shades of yellow we find **lemon**, a warm color, which has the potential to nourish the brain so that you can project yourself clearly, decide firmly and amplify your memory.*

This color is fabulous to help you in studies, analysis, and spelling. It not only stimulates the brain, but cleanses, as it contains a shade of green in its spectrum.

The lemon pushes toxins outside so they can be purified. Lemon yellow collaborates when abdominal spasms, loss of appetite, bone pain, rashes, poor digestion, epidermal rashes, and other skin diseases must be healed.

Lucky Amulets

These Good Luck amulets can help you have a year 2023 full of blessings at home, work, with your family, attract money and health. For the amulets to work properly you should not lend them to anyone else, and you should always have them at hand.

Aries

A frog.

An amulet that will bring you peace, material prosperity and spiritual abundance.

In ancient times, for the Romans and Egyptians, frogs were a symbol of protection, and they used figures of this animal as a talisman.

In Ancient Egypt, frog amulets represented reincarnation, and material abundance; it was a symbol of their goddesses, and they are specifically related to the reincarnation rituals of Osiris, the most important god of the Egyptian pantheon.

The Mayans respected frogs very much, for them they meant happiness, and the Japanese keep them in their purses so that the money that goes always returns. In the art of feng shui, the frog symbolizes abundance and positive powers on all levels.

Candle Colors for Rituals

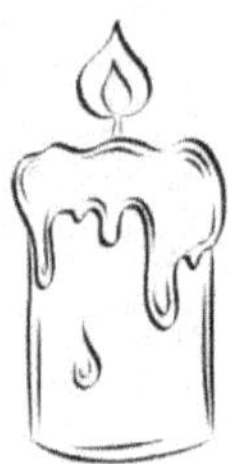

The color of the candle that we are going to use in our rituals is important. All colors have vibration; therefore, they influence a certain area of our lives.

It is essential to know what you want to transform in your life, or what kind of ritual you are going to do, so that you correctly choose a candle that agrees with it.

Yellow: By nature, it is the color of intelligence. A yellow candle is used to stimulate the powers of the mind. In rituals whose purpose is to transmit joy to someone, or something. It is the color of the Sun, vitality, and the desire to live. It is a candle used in situations of sadness. It is used to sweeten moody behaviors. For rituals related to work, studies, and love.

Orange: Contains the energy of red and yellow. It is ideal for attracting harmony, money, and joy. It helps us make decisions. Orange has a dynamic energy so it will be especially useful to enhance any ritual we are doing.

Blue: *It is spectacular to dispel tensions, conflicts, or any difficult situation between people. To connect with the spiritual world, for rituals of love and work.*

White and Gold: *They are beneficial to attract positive energies. They replace the other candles, especially the white one, by containing all the colors in it. Most rituals can be done exclusively with white candles.*

Red: *They are the most used in love spells, since they represent the color of the blood and heart, although they serve in spells related to health and physical strength. They serve as channelers to activate any energy that is stagnant.*

Pink: *Its vibration is higher than red because it is mixed with white. They represent pure love and romanticism. It is the color of compassion and empathy.*

Green: *Color of fertility. It attracts balance to the mind, body, and spirit. It is a color associated with health; it can be used to solve disease situations. Especially useful in rituals, or ceremonies, related to finances or prosperity.*

Purple and Purple: *It is the result of the mixture of red and blue. For rituals related to finances and success.*

Silver and gray: *They are neutral colors; they are between black and white. They are used to neutralize some evil. The silver candles are related to the energy of the night and the Moon, for that reason they are used in rituals or night ceremonies because they are related to that energy.*

Brown: This color is related to the soil, especially when it has not yet been planted. We must be careful when we use it because it can attract uncertainty, so when it is used, you must specify very well what you want, lest we obtain effects contrary to the request. It is used in business rituals.

Black: *It is used in necromancy rites, and to summon negative entities. They help dissolve obstacles. It benefits casual loves. They have a melancholic influence and that is why you must be incredibly careful with their use. They help to release karmic debts and get rid of sorcery and black magic works.*

Why Don't My Spells Work?

There are infinite reasons why a spell may not work, and that is that without realizing it we make mistakes. The energy of rituals is wasted if many people know what you are doing. If you like to perform magic you are not spreading it, you must save your energy for the rituals you are going to practice. This era and is one of the most important rules of sorcerers.

It is especially important to have defined what is the goal or purpose of the ritual or spell, since that will give vitality to the work we are doing. When we begin to work with magic, we must know exactly what purpose we want to achieve. We must be able to summarize our purpose in a single logical sentence.

We must make sure that we have all the components that we are going to need and that these are free of negative energies. Every ritual has a list for its preparation, but you must remember that we can make replacements, if you find some element you can replace it with another, and this will perform the same purpose.

Our mood is key, our emotions must be balanced, and we must feel safe and optimistic. There should not be the slightest possibility that we want to harm another person. The outcome of a ritual depends a lot on you. It is essential that your emotions are in tune with the method, for example: if you want money assume that you will acquire it in large sums. The approach influences the outcome.

To achieve positive results, we must practice them at the right time.

These magical periods are related to astrology, and we must know them and schedule our rituals for these periods of time that will be the most appropriate to perform our magic.

You should not simultaneously perform spells of the same type, because this causes a crossing of energies. Focus on just one for the good result, for the simple fact of trying, you will no longer be working properly, the mere idea of performing others is already enough to weaken the first ritual. The most sensible thing is to reinforce the first job.

Never perform magic for the sake of experimenting, which could cause difficulties in your daily life, as it can incite strange energies.

In special circumstances, such as urgent situations, the ritual is repeated at least three times, on consecutive days in the same week, at designated Earth time, and in some cases three times on the same day, but always at the appropriate times.

The four cardinal points are basic to obtain good results in the practice of magic. The cardinal points are distinguished by the position of the Sun with respect to the Earth: North, South, East, West.

Nature is guided by these four points, so that to each of them belongs one of the ritual elements. Each possesses unique qualities and energies.

The North is about land, security, and consistency. It is a feminine and fertile energy. It is symbolized through green. It is connected to health and the power of the physical. This point favors money rituals and success.

The West corresponds to water, is emotional, sensitive, usually represented by blue. The practices dedicated to this cardinal point activate all kinds of issues.

The South is fire, it shows energy, psychic activities, passion, and desire. It is a masculine energy. It corresponds to the color red.

The East represents the air, is associated with intellect, creativity, abstraction, and mental faculties. It is a masculine energy; its color is yellow.

All elements are paramount in our life, and they have both positive and negative characteristics. It is essential to know them to channel and protect the energies properly.

All magical rituals can begin with an invocation to the cardinal points and the formation of an energy circle within which to invoke the sacred entities. Each of these geographical points has a particular vibration, favorable to know to take advantage of it in our rituals.

The Magic of Time

What day and what time of day are governed by the planet that governs the purpose of the ritual?

Every day has its own concrete energies and its own magic. The secret is to be able to channel these connections in a practical way towards your spells and magical works.

One of the wisdoms most respected by practitioners of magic and esotericism is the benefit of planetary hours, understood as the temporal spaces that are under the energetic influences of a certain planet.

Magical planetary correspondences are simple to use. You must practice how to incorporate them, because it reinforces your magic and the power of your spells. As you begin to study these correspondences, you will realize because before your spells or lucky baths did not work.

Each day has 24 planetary hours, but unlike the hours we traditionally know, they are not restricted to 60-minute periods, it could be.

There are 12 daytime and 12 nighttime planetary hours. Daytime planetary hours extend from sunrise to sunset; while the nocturnal ones go from dusk to dawn the next day.

The daytime planetary hours are used to activate a certain magical intention, while the nocturnal planetary hours because they are permeated with a different type of energy serve to reinforce, during this moment the senses are sharpened.

In addition to using them for our magic work, we can use planetary hours to make the most of our day. In case of having a special day, the signing of an important contract, a trip, a party, a romantic date, the purchase of a house, etc. we will always look for the propitious time in relation to the nature of the planet that best suits us.

According to our calendar, the day starts at 00:00 at night and ends at 00:00 hours the next day. For the astrological and esoteric tradition, the regency of the hours of day and night are shared among the seven planets, from farthest to closest.

*In ancient times, astrologers looked at planets that were distinguishable with the naked eye and recorded the speed of each, from the fastest to the slowest to circle the Earth: **Saturn, Jupiter, Mars, Sun, Venus, Mercury, and the Moon.** And this order is what you must learn to determine which planet rules each hour. (Moon and Sun are luminaries, but astrologers in ancient times ignored it.)*

In the astrological tradition, each hour of the day is governed by a specific planet and the cycle of these hours is what gave name to the Days of the Week. The ancient Chaldeans were the ones who instituted the seven-day calendar, equivalent to the names of the Gods and planets, and named them the same.

They noticed that the length of the days changed according to the seasons, that twice a year, at the Spring and Autumn Equinoxes, the days were equal in length to the nights. For this reason, they divided each 24-hour day into two 12-hour parts.

Daytime hours, ranging from sunrise to sunset.

The night hours, ranging from sunset to sunrise.

The selection of planetary time lies in choosing the most favorable planetary energy for the ritual or spell that we are going to perform.

Sunshine Hour*: It is a spectacular hour for everyone and for all activities, conducive to meetings with influential people (bosses, bank directors, senior executives, etc.), to start a negotiation. To organize our goals, our vocations, our career, to obtain honors.*

To ask for a raise, to make presentations, to speak in public. For spells related to work or money. Rituals related to obtaining promotions and promotions, relationships with superiors and achieving success.

Hour of Venus*: To manifest our creative energy (painting, music, any artistic work). For our health, vitality, and self-esteem. To buy gold and jewelry. Propitious time for feminine issues, to optimize our appearance, go to the hairdresser or receive aesthetic treatments.*

Suitable for shopping, decorating the house, going out with your friends, or having love encounters, having a party, going on a trip, asking for favors, forming a company, and executing investments.

It is the perfect time to ask for marriage and to get married. Also, to make peace after a conflict or a verbal fight. For spells or rituals related to love, contracts, and associations.

Mercury Hour*: In this hour people are more expressive, even the most withdrawn, since Mercury is the planet of communication and, unless it is retrograde, it is favorable to make phone calls, send important correspondences, write, intellectual topics in general, study, undertake short trips, sign contracts, fix your computer and make business deals. Spells of papers, contracts.*

Rituals related to commercial and banking operations; basic or secondary studies, signing contracts and communications, short trips, and alternative medicine.

__Mars Time__: The impulsive nature of Mars will encourage us to be more daring and less prudent, so it is not a good time to start an argument, because it can end in a fight; nor to undertake a trip for the purpose of some transaction, because this hour is prone to accidents, but for any activity in which you need to be more energetic, such as doing exercises, or a situation where courage is needed. It is not good to start a partnership, nor to get married. Remember that Mars always tends to be conflictive.

You can perform spells against enemies, rituals related to bravery, action, and conquest. It is an advisable period for surgical interventions since it favors the healing capacity.

__Moon time__: The emotional, feminine, and nurturing character of the Moon manifests itself in the people and functions of the lunar hour. It is conducive to domestic matters, to talk to mothers and women in general, and to family matters; to deal with the public, cook, eat, wash, and even water the plants; to decorate our house and make it cozier. Family spells or love. Rituals related to the feminine, home and fertility.

__Saturn time__: People seem to be more withdrawn in this hour since the energies of Saturn are always dark, its limiting nature brings problems and delays; it is not advisable to sign contracts, relate socially or start something, however, it is great to start the construction of a house, since Saturn governs *the structures, the bases, and the duration, to buy and sell real estate and land matters. Also, to demolish.*

Excellent time to ask an elderly person for advice. Another beneficial aspect can be organizing, disciplining, and doing tedious work. Great for spells against enemies or to delay something. Rituals related to wisdom and professional studies.

Jupiter Hour*: The beneficial character of Jupiter will be reflected in the people and tasks of this hour. It is favorable to buy travel tickets, for any contact abroad. To gain privileges in enterprise businesses, or start a major activity, start a business, open a business, or to commit.*

To ask favors from people of authority, to obtain honors, to buy real estate. Favorable for money spells and legal matters. Rituals related to prosperity and obtaining jobs. To protect themselves, recover health and start professional studies.

The calculation of planetary hours is affected by the hours of light and shadow you have. The time periods will change depending on the geographical point where you are located and the season of the year (spring, summer, autumn, winter).

To work with the power of planetary hours and enhance your magical rituals you must know the time of sunrise and sunset in your country, and then divide the number of minutes of natural light by 12 (the number of daytime planetary hours).

Bath for the Mercury Retrograde Period

You need three of these plants: Rue, Sage, Rosemary, Lavender, Mint, or Laurel.

Select three of these plants, you can get them in botanicals or esoteric stores. Take a large pot, pour water, and place the plants until they boil completely.

When you have boiled the preparation let it cool. You strain it. Bathe the same way you do daily. After you have bathed, you make the water of the plants from your head and let it run all over your body.

Wait a few seconds before drying for it to penetrate and provide its cleansing effect. Dry yourself, if possible, in the air, without a towel, and you will feel the change in your aura, from that moment you will be ready to practice your spell without risks or sabotage by Mercury Retrograde.

The best times to do rituals related to money are Sundays during the hours of the planet Jupiter, Thursdays during the hours of the Sun or planet Venus and Fridays during the hours of the planet Jupiter. The Moon must be in its crescent phase and in one of these signs: Taurus, Leo, Libra, Sagittarius, or Aquarius.

Rituals for the Sign of Aries

Ritual for Money on the Day of the Solar Eclipse.

Need:
-Ice
- Holy Water
- Corn Kernels
- Sea salt
- 1 clay vessel
- Three green floating sails
- Cartridge paper or parchment and pencil
- 1 new sewing needle

Write your requests about money on paper, then sign your name on the candles with the needle. To cleanse your energy, you will use the clay container where you will place the ice and sacred water, in equal proportions you add three handfuls of sea salt.

Put both hands in the casserole so you will be expelling the negative energies that you have inside you. Take your hands out of the water, but do not dry them out. Add a handful of corn to the bowl and put your hands back in for three minutes.

The last thing you will do is light the candles with wooden matches and place them inside the container. With the fire of the three candles, you burn the paper with your wishes, and you will let the candles burn out.

This ritual must be performed at the exact moment of the Solar Eclipse. The remains of this spell you bury somewhere where the Sun can give you, because in this way your desire will continue to receive energies.

Love Ritual on the Day of the Solar Eclipse

This ritual must be practiced at the exact time that the Solar Eclipse is happening.

Need:
- 2 yellow candles
-Honey
- Pink quartz
- New sewing needle
- Cinnamon essential oil
- 1 Crystal Cup

You must write on each candle your name and the name of the person you love with the needle. Then you consecrate these candles with cinnamon oil.

Place the rose quartz in the crystal cup and pour the honey on it, place the candles on the sides, light them and repeat aloud:

"Nipa agbara ti Eclipse ati agbara agba aye Mo pe awọn ipa ti Agbaye lati fa eniyan yẹn ti o pinnu lati wa ninu igbesi aye mi".

When the candles are consumed, you rinse the quartz and use it as an amulet.

Ritual to Ward Off Relationship Problems

This ritual should be practiced during the Moon Eclipse or in the Full Moon phase.

Need:
- 1 white ribbon
- 1 new scissors
- 1 red ink pen

You should write on the white ribbon with red ink the problem you are having and the name of the person. Then you chop it into seven pieces with the scissors and while you do it you repeat in a loud voice:

"Eyi ni iṣoro mí. Mo fẹ ki o lọ ki o ma pada wa. Jọwọ, mu u kuro lọdọ mí. Bee ni be." You put everything inside a black bag and bury it.

Aztec Spell for Health

Necessary elements.

- *1 white candle.*
- *1 card of the Angel of your devotion.*
- *3 sandalwood incenses.*
- *Vegetable coals.*
- *Dried eucalyptus and basil herbs.*
- *A handful of rice, a handful of wheat.*
- *1 white plate or tray.*
- *8 rose petals pink.*
- *1 bottle of perfume, personal.*
- *1 wooden box.*
-

You should clean the environment by lighting the vegetable coals in a metal container. When the coals are well lit, you will gradually place the dried herbs and walk the room with the container, so that the negative energies are eliminated.

After the incense you must open the windows so that the smoke dissipates. Prepare an altar on top of a table covered with a white tablecloth. Place the chosen card on top of it and around it places the three incenses in the shape of a triangle.

You must consecrate the white candle, then light it and put it in front of the angel together with the uncovered perfume. You must be relaxed, for that you must concentrate on your breathing.

Visualize your angel and thank him for all the good health you have and the one you will always have; this gratitude must come from the depths of your heart.

After you have made the thanks, you will give him as an offering the handful of rice and the handful of wheat, which you must place inside the tray or white plate.

Scatter all the rose petals over the altar, giving thanks again for the favors received. After the thank you will leave the candle lit until it is completely consumed.

The last thing you should do is gather all the remains of candle, incense burners, rice, and wheat, and place them in a plastic bag and throw it in a place where there are trees without the bag.

The angel card along with the rose petals place them inside the box and place it in a safe place in your home.

The energized perfume, you use it will use when you feel that the energies are going down, while you visualize your angel and ask for his protection. This ritual is most effective if you perform it on a Thursday or Monday at the time of Jupiter or the Moon.

Spell to Win in Gambling.

This spell is super effective if you do it on a Friday at the time of the planet Venus or Jupiter.

You should take your wallet or purse and put some coarse sea salt inside. You must also place a high denomination note.

You close the wallet and tie it with a golden ribbon. As you tie it you repeat aloud: "This powerful salt of abundance will multiply my money and attract luck in the game to me." You must leave the wallet for a week under your pillow, after this time you throw the salt on the ground and the bill is left in your wallet (you should not use it to play) next to a sheet of male rue.

Lucky Quartz

We are all attracted to diamonds, rubies, emeralds, and sapphires, obviously they are precious stones. Semiprecious stones such as carnelian, tiger's eye, white quartz, and lapis lazuli are also highly prized as they have been used as ornaments and symbols of power for thousands of years.

What many do not know is that they were valued for more than their beauty: each had a sacred meaning, and their healing properties were as important as their ornamental value.

Crystals still have the same properties today, most people are familiar with the most popular ones such as amethyst, malachite and obsidian, but there are currently new crystals such as larimar, petalite and phenacite that have become known.

A crystal is a solid body with a geometrically regular shape, crystals were formed when the earth was created and have continued to metamorphose as the planet has changed, crystals are the DNA of the earth, they are miniature stores that contain the development of our planet over millions of years.

Some have been subjected to enormous pressures and others grew up in chambers deeply buried underground, others dripped into being. Whatever shape they are, their crystal structure can absorb, conserve, focus and emit energy.

At the heart of the crystal is the atom, its electrons, and protons. The atom is dynamic and is composed of a series of particles that rotate around the center in constant motion, so that, although the crystal may appear motionless, it is a living molecular mass that vibrates at a certain frequency, and this is what gives the energy to the crystal.

The gems used to be a royal and priestly prerogative, the priests of Judaism wore a plaque on the chest full of precious stones which was much more than an emblem to designate their function, because it transferred power to those who used it.

Men have used stones since the stone age since they had a protective function guarding their bearers from various evils. The current crystals have the same power, and we can select our jewelry not only based on their external attractiveness, having them near us can boost our energy (orange carnelian), clean the space around us (amber) or attract wealth (citrine).

Certain crystals such as smoky quartz and black tourmaline could absorb negativity, emit pure and clean energy.

Using a black tourmaline around the neck protects from electromagnetic emanations including that of cell phones, a citrine will not only attract riches, but also help you keep them, place it in the part of the wealth in your home (the left back farthest from the front door). If you are looking for love, crystals can help you, place a rose quartz in the corner of relationships in your house (the right back corner farthest from the front door) its effect is so powerful that it is convenient to add an amethyst to compensate for the attraction.

You can also use rhodochrosite, love will present itself on your way.

Crystals can heal and give balance, some crystals contain minerals known for their therapeutic properties, malachite has a high concentration of copper, wearing a malachite bracelet allows the body to absorb minimal amounts of copper.

Lapis lazuli relieves migraine, but if the headache is caused by stress, amethyst, amber or turquoise located above the eyebrows will relieve it.

Quartz and minerals are jewels of mother earth, give yourself the opportunity, and connect with the magic they give off.

Aries

Smoky quartz

It is a divine symbol on this physical plane. This mystical quartz will give you a lot of light. It is the quartz of mediums, spiritualists, and alchemists as it breaks everything negative. It is associated with the psychic plane, it is the most primitive in the world, and it is an oracle.

It will protect you against the most adverse energies such as envy, anger, and destructive thoughts.

It is the most effective energy healer on the planet, evaporating, increasing, protecting, and molding energy, and is miraculous to unlock it. It transforms energy to the purest admitted state.

It is good for meditation and stimulates memory. On a healing level, it is a therapist, and can be used to balance the chakras. It helps in times of danger and reinforces the solution of these. Psychologically calms fear and helps you with emotional peace. He appeases tragedies and, when he encounters negative emotions, transmutes them.

Consecration of your Amulet or Talisman

It is especially important to consecrate our amulet or talisman to make it work. They must be charged with the five elements, i.e., fire, earth, air, water, and ether (spirit).

*- **Fire**: You must pass your talisman or amulet over the flame of a candle, if it has a pyramidal shape, it is much more powerful. While holding it for several minutes on top of this fire you must repeat in a loud voice:*

"Ego facio in elementis ignis Sicut salamandrae draconem elementa activa viribus curandi potestas et igni".

*- **Earth**: You must bury your amulet or talisman for at least 12 hours in land or sea salt. While burying it you must repeat aloud:*

"Im 'particularum vires terræ loading, per virtutem enim huius terrae magicae gnomes phylacterium fortior sit."

*- **Air**: You must pass to your talisman or amulet the smoke of a palo santo or sage. While you make this incense you must repeat aloud: "Im 'charring caeli elementaribus aquis, silfos sapis atque purissimum elementaris Deneme equitibus"*

*- **Water**: You must put your talisman or amulet inside a container of sacred water, rain, or sea if the material allows it.*

If not, you put the container on top or next to it and leave it like that for 24 hours. While you are accommodating it you repeat in a loud voice:

"Adiuro vos per virtutem aquaeelementaris materia s doque Tellurem cogitationes hominum sensusque malo colligit. humilitatem meam super Devas mandate".

*- **Ether**: You must hold in your hands the talisman or amulet and closing your eyes you repeat in a loud voice: "Ego ferre elementum phasmatis industria, Et impletum est omne desiderium meum numina mala bullas signati".*

In this way you have consecrated your amulet or talisman.

Cleaning your Amulets or Talismans

Your amulets and talismans become contaminated over time and collect negative energies. Your moods also pollute it. That is why it is advisable to clean and recharge them.

There are several methods, and they are all simple:

Amethyst: *You must place the talisman or amulet on or inside a wooden box with amethyst, it will be collecting all the negative energies that it has impregnated.*

Sunlight*: Leave them exposed for 24 hours to sunlight. Those sun's rays are like a magic eraser.*

Moonlight*: You must place your amulet or talisman under the light of the Full Moon, if you can bury them, it is much better.*

Smoke: Pass to your amulet or talisman the smoke of a holy stick or sage.

Sea salt: *Place your amulet or talisman in a container and cover it with sea salt, at least for twelve hours.*

Astrology and Health.

Through the study of the natal chart, we can observe the tendencies to certain diseases since the energy of the zodiacal signs and the planets affect us on a psychological and physical level.

Traditionally, astrology assigns an anatomical equivalence to each zodiac sign. The model is simple since it begins in Aries by the head and goes down to the feet, ruled by Pisces.

Aries, rules the face, eyes, brain, and head. Arians suffer from migraine and headaches. The Aries glands are the adrenals, which push adrenaline into the bloodstream in emergency cases, because of this they have the reputation of impulsive.

Astral Larvae and Energy Parasites

Everything that exists in this world feeds on something. We feed on more solid things, on food that comes from the earth, on animals, and the more subtle entities feed on us, and on our thoughts. It is the way that everyone must survive.

Each of us is possessed of a certain amount of vital energy. That is what makes us live balanced, being in a good state of physical and emotional health. However, many times we realize that our balance is compromised, and that we are not being able to enjoy our life the way we should be able to.

Many can be the causes of our imbalance. However, one of the most recurrent causes is the action of the so-called Astral Larvae.

In places where there is stagnant accumulation of negative energy, such as hospitals, cemeteries, etc. there is a risk of acquiring one of these astral larvae. They are also transmitted during the sexual act, because in it there is not only an exchange of fluids, but also an emotional exchange and energies.

These parasites feed on the vital energy of people who are going through a moment of physical or psychological weakness, as well as those who normally perform magical processes that demand a large amount of energy.

The methods that astral larvae use to feed vary according to some characteristics. To begin with, the size of the larva. It is more common to find young or small larvae, it can also happen that we face real monsters of considerable dimensions.

Small astral larvae tend to jump from one host body to another very frequently, usually by the time they have managed to absorb much of their victim's life energy.

The larger the larvae, as expected, the greater the danger they pose. They could feed on their victim in a much more aggressive way, until leaving it completely empty. The major astral larvae will only change prey in case of the death of the person, or by a victim that offers them a greater source of food.

People who are falling victim to these parasites report a feeling of constant tiredness that does not seem to be improved even taking care of the hours of sleep, feeding, or practicing regular exercise. In addition, they are faced with the continuous presence of negative thoughts.

Many even say they suspect that they do not belong to them, because they are not common thoughts in them. It is normal in victims of astral larvae the frequent development of emotional reactions such as aggression, fear, depression, anger, shame, and discomfort.

General fatigue also causes a decrease in the immune system, which predisposes the host to the development of other symptoms that in other circumstances could not occur in the body.

The emission of energy that this state causes makes the person the specific source that the larva seeks for its development.

What are they?

Energy parasites, also called entities, are etheric or astral fragments, elemental beings, energies, etc., that have adhered to us through different channels, being the main ones during pregnancy, during our childhood and especially, when we find low energies, or low level of vibrations.

These energy parasites feed on our vital energy, feeding on our fears and frustrations, consuming us little by little. Some of the diseases that appear in our physical body, including cancer, have been generated by these energy parasites.

Where are they staying?

These parasites can lodge in the physical, etheric, and astral bodies. In the physical body, they are usually lodged in the head, in the areas: dorsal, lumbar, and sacral of the back, in the iliac area, in the vagina or uterus, in the colon, etc., in general in any internal cavity. Usually, the energetic parasites that lodge in our physical body, are attracted to the positively charged elements of our body, staying in our bone system.

How are they detected?

First, these energetic parasites produce some cravings that force us to consume excessively. Among the cravings we find the following: Sweets and chocolates, heavy foods such as meats and spicy foods, coffee, tobacco, junk food, alcohol and mostly sugar.

Its presence is also manifested by back pain, between the shoulder blades or the lumbar area, in addition to excessive tiredness, difficulty sleeping, blurred vision, the feeling of having an extra weight on our back, like as if a backpack were carried.

As this has no visible manifestation, the presence of astral larvae is rarely detected by people who have not been trained for this. However, they always manifest internally.
Sleep problems and nightmares are common. Some people have reported a feeling of tightness in the chest, such as a force pressing them down.

The personal mood is aggravated, to the point where unexplained panic attacks and diseases of mysterious origin can occur.

According to experts, forty to sixty percent of the problems that compromise the psyche of the person are related to the participation, even if temporary, of a small larva. And from five to ten percent, astral larvae are responsible for the whole problem.

To protect ourselves from astral larvae you can incur some simple solutions, although as always, it is best to prevent them before they are installed. For that, there are those who recommend limiting the energy body as much as possible. That way, the person can go unnoticed and not attract attention as a potential victim.

It is good to use camphor or lemon to keep them away.

However, if you already know a victim of astral larvae and want to help them, it is important that the size of the larva in question is distinguished.

Astral creatures often take advantage of attacks while people sleep, although there are forces that attack while one is awake and they are too scary things, because it is much stronger. Apart from physical attacks, there are mental attacks, which are much more subtle, and which can be said to be a victim of everyone.

These negative creatures that live in the astral world (world of emotions), feed on our negative emotions, such as anger, fear, sadness, depression, and letting themselves be consumed by these emotions, is to let themselves be consumed by these creatures, and that is why you feel that strong uncontrollable emotion.

Of course, in the same way that we make animal farms and then consume their food, these creatures prepare us on an emotional level to be their food, and it is through provoking negative feelings so that we let ourselves be carried away by them.

Human beings are the only ones who can produce certain types of thoughts and emotions. In this way, someone consumed by fear feeds these creatures, and these creatures somehow cause people to feel certain types of fear.

There are levels and levels in this part, and the person with little willpower, slowly sinks into these negative feelings. Someone starts out as a person who gives him anger, and then *he becomes wilder, more instinctive, until he goes to another level, and becomes a murderer.*

How to protect the House from Larvae or Astral Parasites

- *Allow the entry of light, especially the natural one every morning open the windows and let in the renewal of energy.*
- *Keep your home clean and airy.*
- *Do not accumulate things you do not use.*
- *Do not keep broken things at home.*
- *Do not have old objects at home, unless you know their origin.*
- *Avoid excessive mirrors in the rooms.*
- *Do not play with a Ouija board.*
- *Do not play in abandoned houses or cemeteries.*
- *Do not practice black magic.*
- *Frequently light incense, essences, and candles in your home.*
- *Take water baths with sea salt and vinegar or other types of baths for cleaning the aura. (If you want Sprays to clear the aura visit page www.esoterismomagia.com)*

- Wear quartz or crystals in accessories.

- Have glasses of water with sea salt in the corners of your house under your bed and renew them when they are dirty and have collected bad energies.

-Clean the house from the inside out with sea salt.

- *It is important to have in the house objects such as: Angels, elephants with the trunk up, Buddhas, owls, frogs.*
- *Use Tibetan bowls or metal bells as the sound of these is purifying of aura and energy.*

You must remember that no cleaning will help for a long time, if in the house continues to reign an atmosphere of discussions, lies, offenses, dirt, disorder, vices etc. So, try to keep your frequency vibrating high, this way you will not give opportunity for this type of energies to manifest and adhere to your life and home.

Objects that attract Prosperity.

To eliminate the negative energies that hold us back, you can choose to have different tweaks that attract good luck and prosperity.

*- **Elephant statuette for good luck**. It symbolizes power and strength, attracts good luck and wisdom to the home. The perfect place to place this amulet is the entrance hallway to the house, looking inward, welcoming prosperity, and letting it in.*

*- **Bamboos for prosperity.** To attract success and prosperity, Asians claim that bamboo is excellent.*

*- **Horse horseshoe.** It is one of the most popular talismans to attract luck. Its semicircular shape is linked to fertility and the iron with which it is made to power. To make it work as an amulet, it is advisable to hang it on the door, with the ends facing up.*

In this way, it becomes a receptacle of astral forces. Ideally, you should look for a horseshoe with seven holes, since that is the ancestral number that is associated with good fortune.

*- **Fish**. The goldfish is one of the eight sacred symbols of Buddha, as such it is considered a talisman of wealth and*

good luck. But it does not have to be just golden. Fish figures can also be silver, crystal or even carved in wood, and can be left inside the home, or used in jewelry. Not only do they attract good energy, but they also protect the wearer from bad luck.

*- **Cat of fortune.** This talisman of Japanese origin is one of the best known in the West. The kitten with his hand raised as a sign invites good energies to enter the house or place. The cat can be placed anywhere in the house that is visible, but facing the door is excellent.*

*- **Eye of Horus**. This traditional amulet of the Egyptian civilization is used since ancient times, to deactivate envy and the "evil eye". It is also believed to drive away disease. It is normal to find two versions of the eye: the left one that symbolizes the Moon, and the right, which represents the Sun. The latter is the one to which the good energies are assigned.*

*- **Smiling Buddha**. Having in the house the figure of a smiling Buddha produces wealth, prosperity, and money. It also transforms the energies of the house, so that peace and good humor predominate.*

*- **Turtle.** The turtle represents health, longevity, stability, and balance, having them as pets augurs' prosperity. Having the statuette of a turtle carrying its young on its back represents the good opportunities that will appear to us in the future.*

    - **Candelabra.** *The candlestick must have seven arms, belongs to the Hebrew tradition, and is considered as a lucky charm for happiness and balance in the home. Even in the esoteric world it represents a light in the darkness. To attract abundance and luck to the home you should hang a miniature chandelier behind the front door of your house.*

    - **The Turkish eye**. *Historically it has served to dissolve the evil eye. If you place him facing the door, he is the bearer of good luck in the house, and acts as a protector against evil and bad energies.*

    - **Four-leaf clover.** *It is the good luck charm par excellence, although it is a rare specimen that only occurs once in 10,000 cases. Each leaf of the clover represents an element of happiness: love, health, fortune, or prosperity.*

    - **Old keys**. *Old keys bring good luck, especially to the economy of home, business, and work. They symbolize the opening of doors, that is, new opportunities.*

    - **The bells.** *They fill the home with good vibrations and favor the circulation of good energies, removing the negative* *ones and attracting the positive ones. They are usually placed on doors or in patios.*

*- **The dice**. They symbolize the future and good luck. You must always carry one with you in your wallet, purse or loose in your bag.*

*- **The Hand of Fatima.** In some cultures, it is considered a bearer of good luck, abundance, and health.*

*- **Las Cruces.** The cross of Caravaca, the Egyptian and the Celtic are crosses considered protective against diseases. They also attract prosperity.*

*- **Wind cheeks**. They are famous for attracting positive energy, in fact, they are also called "communicators of angels".*

*- **Rabbit's leg**. Widely used in Western culture, it is one of the most popular and oldest lucky amulets for the home.*

*- **Blue color**. It symbolizes the water element, so it creates fluidity. If you lose your money easily, add this color to your home.*

*- **Quartz.** Selenite, white quartz, and black tourmaline are excellent choices for crystals that attract good energies.*

Use them as decoration pieces and be sure to leave them overnight in a window so that they are charged with energy from the moonlight.

*- **Dolphin figure**. The stories about the good luck that dolphins attract are incredibly old and come from sailors and people who work at sea.*

Objects that Obstruct Prosperity.

*- **Unwanted ornaments or gifts.** You should not keep items given to you by people you dislike or someone with whom you abruptly or problematically broke off a relationship.*

*- **Dried flowers, artificial plants, or ashes of someone deceased**. Vase with withered flowers or ornaments with dried flowers are usually of bad omen. The same goes for artificial plants and flowers and the ashes of a dead person, since, having no life, they do not let energy flow and interfere negatively with the energy balance of the home.*

*- **Cactus or thorny plants**. Cactus or thorny plants should not be at home as they can attract economic problems.*

-   ***Broken or stained mirrors***. *The mirrors should always look clean, if they are broken or in poor condition you should throw them away. According to Feng shui they should never be placed in front of the foot of the bed.*

- *The broom* *up. When you store the broom in the toilet, you should not put it with the bristles up, this is synonymous with bad luck and drives money away. You must always have it down.*

- *Parts of dead animals.* *Having dead animal parts at home, such as skins, shells, horns, ivories, snails, or stuffed species are equivalent to bad luck. Belief has to do with stagnant energies. You will have death present in your home.*

- *Clothes left or in poor condition.* *It is especially important to avoid the accumulation of old or broken clothes that we no longer use. They are an obstacle that do not allow to renew the energies of the home.*

- *Place a fish tank in the kitchen or bedroom*. *If you have a fish tank in the kitchen or bedroom you are making a serious mistake. According to Feng Shui, those areas require more the presence of the fire element and water could annihilate it.*

- ***An old calendar.*** *Tradition says that showing the wrong year, month or day is a reminder of the time that passes, and this will negatively damage your life by attracting bad luck.*

- ***A stopped clock****. A watch stopped or simply not working, it is better that you throw it, according to Chinese tradition, attract bad luck because time stopped on them. In addition, it is a sign of a shorter life.*

- ***Photos of natural disasters.*** *Photos in your home showing natural disasters are symbols of bad luck. Not only images of death or destruction, but also photos of snowfall or rain.*

- ***A black door.*** *(Not if you look north). According to Feng Shui, a black gate facing south, east, or west invites bad luck.*

- ***Umbrellas or umbrellas inside the house.*** *It is one of the oldest known superstitions of ill omen. An umbrella does not give bad luck or is not a symbol of it, however when one is opened inside the house, or any interior, it is said to attract bad fortune.*

- ***An axe inside the house.*** *The axe inside the home is not only an object of bad luck, but also of death.*

What is the safest sign of the zodiac?

Self-confidence helps us be prepared to face life's obstacles. When we have security, if things do not work out, self-confidence helps us try again. Self-confidence or self-confidence is often confused with self-esteem, and although they are connected, they are not the same.

Self-esteem is a person's general appreciation of themselves, and self-confidence describes the estimation of one's ability to execute a goal.

Not all zodiac signs have the same level of security, there are some that are super insecure, however, others have an incredible level of perseverance and self-confidence.

Aries: thinks that asking for help is an indication of inferiority, does not recognize their limitations. Asking for help is brave and self-confident people.

Taurus: He hates stepping out of his comfort zone. By not expanding your boundaries for fear of situations that represent a new challenge, you are sabotaging your self-confidence.

Gemini: tends to value their actions as negative. They become overwhelmed by seeking the approval of others, which is a symptom of insecurity.

Cancer: sees its defects, but not its virtues. Negative thoughts about your abilities are lack of personal security.

Leo: It is aggressively safe. They do not feel an obligation to do things a certain way, they attack the problem in the way that seems most convenient to them. This is called security.

Virgo: They love to have the approval of others, sacrificing their true personality. This need for approval is synonymous with "I don't trust myself."

Libra: does not risk for fear of failure, or having chosen incorrectly, forgetting that planned spontaneity does not exist. By equating what is worth to your failures or successes, you are eternally condemning yourself to have no security.

Scorpio: They are motivated by their desire to grow and whenever they are given the option to do so, they feel confident in themselves. They have no room to feel doubts.

Sagittarius: does not believe in circumstances, they go in search of the circumstances they want, and if they do not find them, they manufacture them. They are self-confident and willing to be disapproved of by others because they are confident in their own abilities.

Capricorn: they mask their insecurity by being competitive because this way they avoid feeling like failures. He tolerates failure very badly and always justifies his mistakes, instead of accepting them and learning from them.

Aquarius: they do not tolerate that anything associated with them is less than perfect. This self-demand and constant search for a perfection that does not exist is an expression of insecurity.

Pisces: suffers from personal insecurity, a type of insecurity that feeds on low self-esteem. This insecurity is a consequence of making a decision that generated negative consequences, and from this Pisces experience I conclude that you cannot trust your criteria to make decisions.

Self-assurance is healing, as being sure of who we are and our abilities allows us not to be enslaved to the opinions of others, and to constantly seek recognition from others. It is a process by which we must value each achievement achieved, forgetting negative criticism or manipulations of others, always relying on our strengths.

Start building your security today and you will see how good you will feel.

Bibliography

Some information was extracted from the books published by the authors: Love for All Hearts, Money for All Pockets and Horoscope 2022 and 2023.

Articles written in the Nuevo Herald by one of the writers are included in this book.

About the Authors

In addition to her astrological knowledge, Alina Rubi has an abundant professional education; She holds certifications in Psychology, Hypnosis, Reiki, Bioenergetic Healing with Crystals, Angelic Healing, Dream Interpretation and is a Spiritual Instructor. Rubi has knowledge of Gemology, which he uses to program stones or minerals and turn them into powerful Amulets or Talismans of protection.

Rubi has a practical and purposeful character, which has allowed it to have a special and integrating vision of several worlds, facilitating solutions to specific problems. Alina writes the Monthly Horoscopes for the website of the American Association of Astrologers; you can read them on the www.astrologers.com website. At this moment he writes a weekly column in the newspaper El Nuevo Herald on spiritual topics, published every Sunday in digital form and on Mondays in print. He also has a program and weekly horoscope on the YouTube channel of this newspaper. His Astrological Yearbook is published every year in the newspaper "Diario las Américas", under the column Rubi Astrologa.

Rubi has authored several articles on astrology for the monthly publication "Today's Astrologer", has taught

Astrology, Tarot, Hand Reading, Crystal Healing, and Esotericism. She has weekly videos on esoteric topics on her YouTube channel: Rubi Astrologa. She had her own astrology program broadcast daily through Flamingo T.V., has been interviewed by several TV and radio programs, and every year her "Astrological Yearbook" is published with the horoscope sign by sign, and other interesting mystical topics.

She is the author of the books "Rice and Beans for the Soul" Part I, II, and III, a compilation of esoteric articles, published in English, Spanish, French, Italian and Portuguese. "Money for All Pockets", "Love for All Hearts", "Health for All Bodies, Astrological Yearbook 2021, Horoscope 2022, Rituals and Spells for Success in 2022, Spells and Secrets, Astrology Classes, Rituals and Amulets 2023 and Chinese Horoscope 2023 all available in five languages: English, Italian, French, Japanese and German.

Rubi speaks English and Spanish perfectly, combines all her talents and knowledge in her readings. He currently resides in Miami, Florida.

*For more information you can **visit the website** www.esoterismomagia.com*

Alina A. Rubi is the daughter of Alina Rubi. She is currently studying psychology at Florida International University.

As a child she was interested in all metaphysical, esoteric subjects, and practices astrology, and Kabbalah from the age of four. He has knowledge of Tarot, Reiki, and Gemology. She is not only the author, but editor along with her sister Angeline A. Rubi, of all the books published by her and her mother.

For more information you can contact her by email: **rubiediciones29@gmail.com**

www.ingramcontent.com/pod-product-compliance
Lightning Source LLC
Chambersburg PA
CBHW080909160726
48000CB00009B/2923